Galileo
and the Telescope

Yoming S. Lin

PowerKiDS
press.
New York

To Dave, my big huggable teddy bear. I love that we get to learn about the world together.

Published in 2012 by The Rosen Publishing Group, Inc.
29 East 21st Street, New York, NY 10010

First Edition

Editor: Amelie von Zumbusch
Book Design: Greg Tucker

Photo Credits: Cover (Galileo), p. 20 (top left) Imagno/Getty Images; cover (telescope), pp. 11 (left), 18 SSPL/Getty Images; p. 4 Stock Montage/Getty Images; p. 5 Vincenzo Pinto/AFP/Getty Images; p. 6 SuperStock/Getty Images; pp. 7 (top, bottom), 11 (right), 15 (Sun, Venus, Earth), 20 (bottom left) Shutterstock.com; p. 8 © www.iStockphoto.com/Hulton Archive; pp. 9, 20 (top right) Wikimedia Commons; p. 10 Hulton Archive/Thinkstock; p. 12 AbleStock.com/Thinkstock; p. 14 Photos.com/Getty Images; pp. 16–17, 21 Peter Willi/Getty Images; p. 19 Jess Alford/Getty Images; p. 20 (bottom right) Mansell/Time & Life Pictures/Getty Images.

Library of Congress Cataloging-in-Publication Data

Lin, Yoming S.
 Galileo and the telescope / by Yoming S. Lin. — 1st ed.
    p. cm. — (Eureka!)
 Includes index.
 ISBN 978-1-4488-5030-3 (library binding)
1. Galilei, Galileo, 1564-1642—Juvenile literature. 2. Astronomers—Italy—Biography—Juvenile literature. 3. Telescopes—Juvenile literature. I. Title.
 QB36.G2L657 2012
 520.92—dc22
 [B]
                                              2010050104

Manufactured in the United States of America

CPSIA Compliance Information: Batch #WS11PK: For Further Information contact Rosen Publishing, New York, New York at 1-800-237-9932

Contents

Galileo's View of the Universe

Have you ever looked into the sky and wondered what was out there? Galileo Galilei did. Galileo was a scientist. He lived hundreds of years ago in Italy.

Galileo invented a telescope to look at the sky. This tool made faraway objects, such as planets, look bigger

Unlike most other scientists, Galileo is most often known by just his first name. He is shown holding his telescope in this picture.

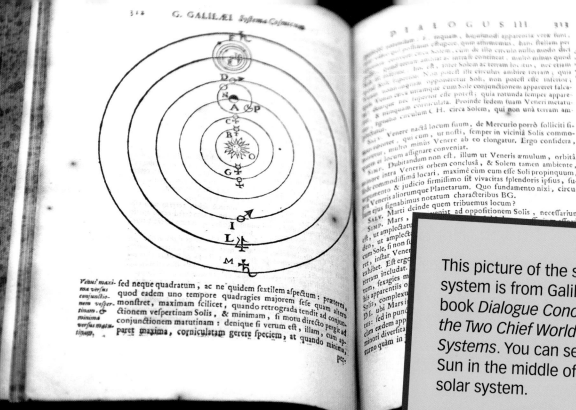

and closer. He used it to see things in the sky that had never been seen before.

At that time, most people believed that Earth was at the center of the universe. They thought that everything **revolved**, or moved, around it. The things Galileo saw with his telescope proved that Earth and the other planets really travel around the Sun.

Galileo was born on February 15, 1564, in Pisa, Italy. He came from a noble family. They did not have much money, though. His parents were named Giulia and Vincenzo. Galileo had six brothers and sisters. When Galileo was young, his family moved to Florence.

Galileo's father was a musician. He played the lute, as the musician in this painting is doing. He wrote music and studied sound, too.

As a teenager, Galileo told his father that he wanted to be a monk. His father was not happy with this idea. In 1581, Galileo began to study at the **University** of Pisa, a school in Pisa. He studied both math and medicine. His father wanted him to be a doctor. Galileo's favorite subject was math, though.

Top: Pisa is known for its leaning tower. The tower is the bell tower of Pisa's cathedral. *Bottom*: Florence is known for the big dome of its cathedral.

After Galileo finished his studies, he became a teacher at the University of Pisa. Several years later, he moved to Padua. He taught math and **astronomy**, the study of things in the sky, at the university there.

Galileo had a busy family life, too. In 1591, Galileo's father died. Galileo was the oldest son,

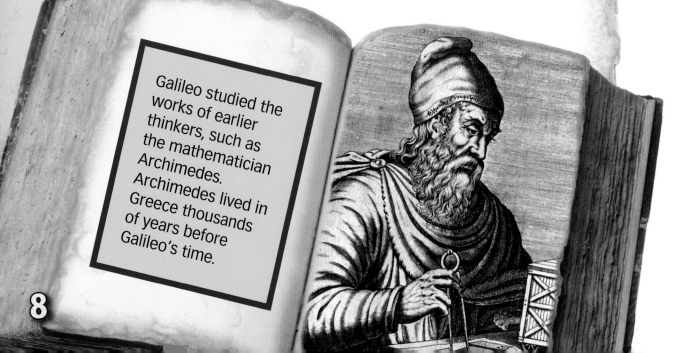

Galileo studied the works of earlier thinkers, such as the mathematician Archimedes. Archimedes lived in Greece thousands of years before Galileo's time.

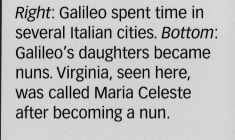
Right: Galileo spent time in several Italian cities. *Bottom*: Galileo's daughters became nuns. Virginia, seen here, was called Maria Celeste after becoming a nun.

Milan

Padua

Pisa

Florence

ITALY

Rome

Sardinia

Mediterranean Sea

Sicily

so he had to help take care of his brothers and sisters. In 1600, Galileo had his first child with Marina Gamba. They would have three children together. They named their daughters Virginia and Livia. Their son was called Vincenzio.

9

Galileo's Science Experiments

In Pisa and Padua, Galileo did many science experiments. Do you think a watermelon would fall faster than an apple? Many people would guess that heavy objects fall faster than light ones. Galileo tested this by dropping different things from the same height.

Stories say that Galileo dropped heavy and light weights off the Leaning Tower of Pisa. This showed that things of different weights fall at the same speed.

Left: This pendulum clock is based on plans Galileo left.
Right: Galileo invented a thermometer, or a tool to measure heat, that used different kinds of liquids.

He saw that heavy and light things hit the ground at the same time.

Galileo also experimented with **pendulums**. Pendulums have one fixed end and one end that swings back and forth. Galileo discovered that no matter how high a pendulum swings, it takes the same amount of time for it to swing from one side to another. This meant pendulums could be used to measure time.

The Great Telescope

In 1609, Galileo learned about telescopes. They had just been invented in the Netherlands. These telescopes were tubes with pieces of curved glass, called **lenses**, at each end. People looked through a lens called the **eyepiece**. The **objective lens** was pointed at objects.

The telescopes Galileo used were much simpler than the telescopes that people use today.

Eyepiece

Objective lens

In this drawing, you can see how light moves through the kind of telescope that Galileo made. Each lens bends the light in a different way.

The lenses bent light that entered the telescope. This made objects seen through the telescope look closer.

Galileo soon made his own, better telescope. He used math to figure out how strong to make each lens. His telescope **magnified** things 20 times. This means it made things look 20 times bigger. Galileo was the first person to use a telescope to look at objects in the sky.

The ancient Greek scientist Aristotle said that everything revolved around Earth. People believed this for nearly 2,000 years. Then, in 1543, the Polish scientist Nicolaus Copernicus suggested that Earth and other planets circled the Sun. However, he could not prove this.

Galileo used his telescope to show that Copernicus was right. In 1610, Galileo saw four moons traveling around Jupiter with his

Nicolaus Copernicus lived between 1473 and 1543. His book *De Revolutionibus* argued that Earth and other planets circled the Sun.

14

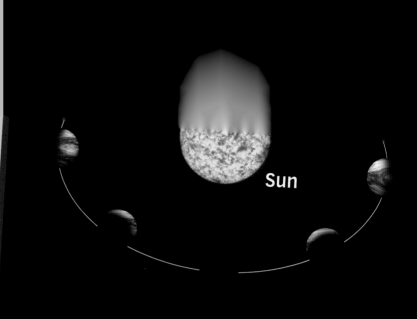

In this drawing, you can see eight of the phases Venus goes through in its path around the Sun as seen from Earth.

Sun

Earth

telescope. This proved that everything did not revolve around Earth. Galileo also saw that Venus goes through **phases**. This means that how Venus looks from Earth changes throughout the year. The way Venus's shape changed showed that Venus revolved around the Sun, not Earth.

Galileo Gets in Trouble

During Galileo's life, the **Catholic Church** had lots of power. It taught that Earth was at the center of the universe. In the 1630s, Galileo wrote a book about his discoveries. It stated the idea that Earth moved around the Sun. The church

believed he was spreading **heresy**. Heresy is going against a faith's teachings.

Galileo was Catholic. He argued that his beliefs were not against the church. In 1633, Galileo was called to Rome to face the Catholic Church. He pleaded guilty of heresy. The church told Galileo that he could not leave his home for the rest of his life.

This painting by Joseph-Nicolas Robert-Fleury shows Galileo's trial. Galileo was tried by the Inquisition. This was a part of the Catholic Church that tried to root out heresy.

17

The Father of Modern Science

Galileo died in Arcetri, Italy, in 1642. He will always be remembered for using his telescopes to show that the planets revolve around the Sun. He changed the way people look at the universe.

Galileo is also known as the first scientist to use math in his experiments. He is considered the first person to use

This exact copy of one of Galileo's telescopes was made in 1923 in Florence. This telescope makes things look 21 times bigger.

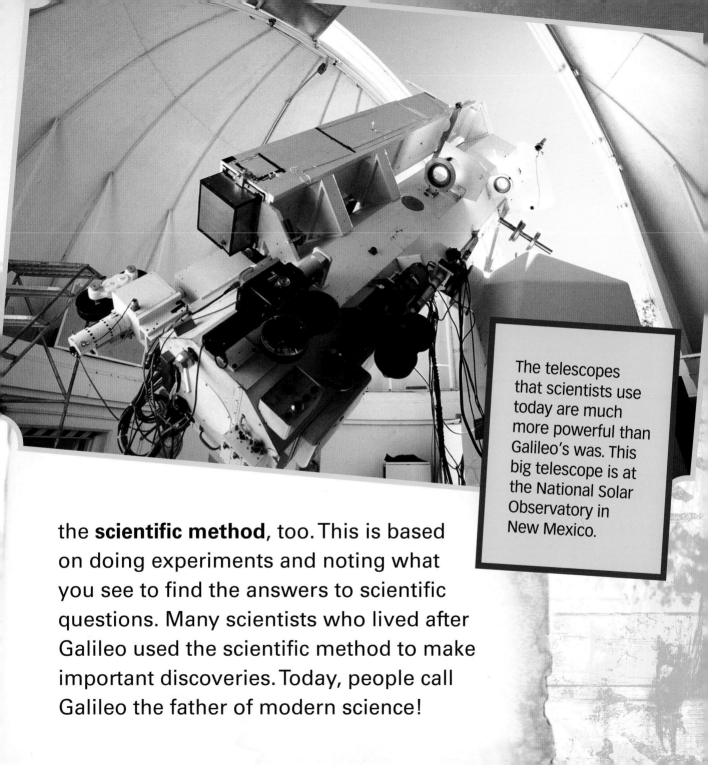

The telescopes that scientists use today are much more powerful than Galileo's was. This big telescope is at the National Solar Observatory in New Mexico.

the **scientific method**, too. This is based on doing experiments and noting what you see to find the answers to scientific questions. Many scientists who lived after Galileo used the scientific method to make important discoveries. Today, people call Galileo the father of modern science!

Timeline

On October 15, 1582, Italy switched calendars to the one we use today. The dates noted here from before that time come from the older Julian calendar.

December 1592

Galileo begins to teach math at the University of Padua.

August 1600

Galileo's daughter Virginia is born. She is his first child.

September 1581

Galileo enters the University of Pisa.

1550   1560   1570   1580   1590   1600

February 15, 1564

Galileo is born in Pisa, Italy.

1597

Galileo invents his military compass and teaches people how to use it. A compass is a tool for measuring angles.

January 1610

Galileo sees four moons revolving around Jupiter.

April 30, 1633

Galileo pleads guilty of heresy.

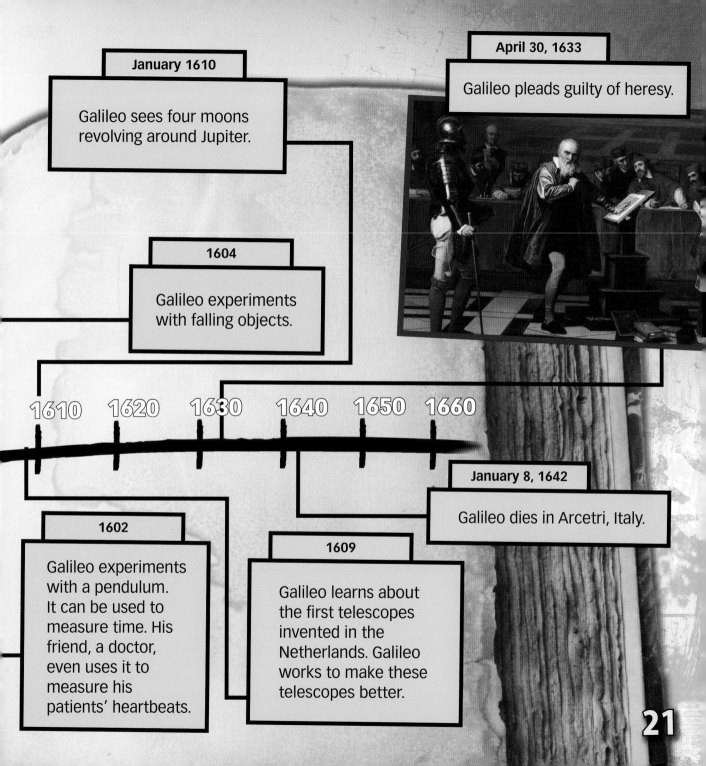

1604

Galileo experiments with falling objects.

1610　1620　1630　1640　1650　1660

January 8, 1642

Galileo dies in Arcetri, Italy.

1602

Galileo experiments with a pendulum. It can be used to measure time. His friend, a doctor, even uses it to measure his patients' heartbeats.

1609

Galileo learns about the first telescopes invented in the Netherlands. Galileo works to make these telescopes better.

Inside the Science

1. You see things when light **reflects**, or shines back, off them. The light enters your eye, where the eye's lens bends it to make a picture. Galileo's telescope worked in much the same way. However, it also had a second lens to make the picture look bigger.

2. Galileo's telescope was a refracting telescope. Its lenses bent light and made things look bigger. Reflecting telescopes were invented later. They use mirrors to reflect light to make objects look larger.

3. Lenses that curve in are called concave lenses. Those that curve out are convex lenses. Galileo's telescope used an objective lens that was flat on one side and convex on the other. The eyepiece had one concave side and one flat side.

4. Venus is not the only object in the sky that goes through phases when looked at from Earth. The Moon does, too. Some of these phases are full moon, half moon, and crescent moon.

5. Since Galileo's time, scientists have found many more moons around Jupiter. They are still finding more!

Glossary

astronomy (uh-STRAH-nuh-mee) The science of the Sun, the Moon, planets, and stars.

Catholic Church (KATH-lik CHURCH) A church whose leader is called the pope and that teaches that Jesus Christ is the Son of God.

eyepiece (EYE-pees) The part of a telescope through which people look.

heresy (HER-eh-see) Going against the beliefs held by a faith.

lenses (LENZ-ez) Clear, curved parts of the eye or pieces of glass that focus light.

magnified (MAG-nuh-fyd) Made an object appear larger than it is.

objective lens (ub-JEK-tiv LENZ) The curved glass in a telescope that faces the object being looked at.

pendulums (PEN-juh-lumz) Tools that have one fixed end and one end that swings back and forth.

phases (FAYZ-ez) The different shapes of an object in space as seen from Earth.

reflects (rih-FLEKTS) Throws back light, heat, or sound.

revolved (rih-VOLVD) Circled around.

scientific method (sy-en-TIH-fik MEH-thud) The system of running experiments in science.

university (yoo-neh-VER-seh-tee) A school for higher learning.

Index

Web Sites

Due to the changing nature of Internet links, PowerKids Press has developed an online list of Web sites related to the subject of this book. This site is updated regularly. Please use this link to access the list:
www.powerkidslinks.com/eure/galileo/